# ESTR FROM ADULT CHILDREN

How to Reconnect with your Estranged Children and Get Your Family Back Together. Best Ways to Have that Healing Conversation with Your Estranged Daughter/Son

---

## ANGELINA MARSH

# Table of Contents

*Page left Intentionally*

# Introduction

If you are estranged from your adult child, if your child has cut you out of his or her life; whether for a long or short time, it is a gut-wrenching experience. When your child cuts you out of his/her life it provokes deep feelings of shame, guilt, bewilderment, and hurt, all of which can easily turn to anger. On top of that, it can also arouse people's worst suspicions and leave you feeling judged, even by friends and family.

Sometimes, of course, there are circumstances in which cutting off from a parent is the only viable option for an adult child (age 18 and older), for instance, in the case of past or present physical, emotional or sexual abuse from a parent.

While it's common to pin the reason for the estrangement on everything from money issues, to personality conflicts, to divorce or difficult family dynamics, many times, though, estranged parents are left in the dark trying to figure out what went wrong.

And when you are in the dark, the easiest thing to blame is yourself; to believe that you failed as a parent.

But here's the reality: it was not your choice to sever the relationship. Although you may have contributed to the tensions between you, you are not responsible for your child's choice to cut you off.

These are common scenarios we find ourselves in as parents and children and there is a need to first understand the situation and then go ahead to get probable solutions to the problem.

This book is specially made for estranged parents but it has also been structured to be of good use to children too. Hence, it is for everyone and it contains a whole lot of insights into the feeling of being estranged.

Get busy with this book, and learn how to get out of that estranged position.

Happy reading!

# CHAPTER 1

# Estrangement in its entirety!

Estrangement refers to a broken or disrupted family relationship in which family members have reduced or stopped communicating and interacting with each other. Usually a gradual process rather than a single event, estrangement often involves periods of distance mixed with times of reconciliation. Estrangement can impact mental health and well-being, but therapy can help you cope and, if desired, reconnect with family members.

## What Does Estranged Mean?

To be estranged means to experience distance or separation from others, such as family members, with notable diminish in or even complete loss of contact with people with whom you once had close relationships. Estrangement is considered to be a loss of a family relationship that was originally at least somewhat nurturing.

Estrangement is typically a process rather than a single event. When at least one family member desires to separate themselves from another, usually because of a prolonged negative relationship or pattern of problematic interactions, they begin to distance themselves physically and emotionally, withdrawing from support and interdependence.

A *schism* between family members is complex and often cyclical, with periods of separation and reconciliation. This can be incredibly difficult, causing added confusion, stress, anxiety, and disenfranchised grief. Estrangement can vary in length. Reported lengths of separation range from less than six months to more than 30 years.

Estrangement is considered by some experts to be more complicated than divorce because of its lack of finality and closure. Accordingly, being estranged from one or more family members can substantially affect someone's mental health and well-being.

## Effects of Estrangement

Humans depend on family relationships for support, security, and stability; estrangement disrupts this and impacts mental health. Estrangement of a parent and child, even an adult child, involves a loss of the original attachment system, the process that creates emotional bonding and a secure base.

Some research suggests that estrangement destroys the original attachment system, causes pain of rejection, triggers chronic stress, and creates a sense of uncertainty. Together, these feelings can decrease self-esteem and cause a sense of worthlessness, make coping difficult, decrease resilience in the face of other challenges, contribute to anxiety and depression, and damage physical health. The breakage of this secure, once-predictable family bond brings numerous challenges to someone's overall well-being.

Estrangement can cause:

- A sense of grief and loss
- Anxiety, including separation anxiety
- Pervasive sadness
- Loneliness
- Ambiguous loss
- Feelings of being left out or even vilified by other family members
- Negative emotions and mood
- A decreased ability to self-regulate
- Ongoing trust issues in other relationships
- Impacts on other family members, like taking sides or feeling awkward, especially around family events
- A tendency to ruminate about problems in all relationships rather than enjoying positive, nurturing aspects of relationships

One reason estrangement is often so problematic and difficult is that family relationships, especially a parent-child bond, is expected to be permanent with no real option to end it like one might end a friendship, romantic relationship, or marriage.

It's important to note that estrangement doesn't always have an exclusively negative impact on those involved. For some, cutting off communication and distancing from a family member perceived to be toxic can bring relief and a welcome sense of freedom and peace. Many people report decreased stress, increased insight and self-understanding, and feelings of strength and happiness after severing negative ties.

## Signs of Family Estrangement

The process of family estrangement isn't always loud, quick, and understood by all involved. It often happens over time and could even be surprising to some involved in the damaged relationship. Even when it seemingly does happen suddenly, it is often a result of tensions and difficulties that have accumulated over time.

Keep in mind that estrangement isn't usually a single event but instead is a process that exists on a continuum.

People frequently move between separation and reconciliation, making estrangement a fluid process that can be difficult to understand.

The following signs can help you recognize estrangement in one of your family relationships:

- Decreasing communication (both the frequency and meaningful nature of interactions)
- Physical distancing (moving away or avoiding close proximity)
- Reduction in emotional closeness and feelings of connection, caring, and empathy
- Increasing negative emotions and affect (displays of anger, bitterness, and similar emotions)
- Declining relationship effort (choosing not to be connected in typical ways)
- Ignoring role expectations (not behaving according to expectations, such as failing to nurture and support)
- Delegitimizing (officially, and sometimes legally, breaking all ties)

## Causes of Family Estrangement

While the exact cause of family estrangement is highly personal and unique to each person and situation, psychologists have identified common themes. Deep-seated problems and issues from the past can cause rifts in family relationships. Abuse, neglect, favoritism, and lack of support are commonly stated reasons for cutting off family ties. Poor parenting styles may also contribute to ongoing problems long past childhood and can cause estrangement.

The following are common causes of estrangement:

- Differences in values and conflict over life decisions/religious beliefs, gender identity, sexual orientation, chosen romantic partners, and political views
- Money issues
- Clashes over inheritance situations
- Unacknowledged or untreated mental illness in the family
- Substance misuse

- Abuse or bullying among siblings
- A history of estranged relationships
- Combative/easily angered personality types

## What You Can Do to Reconcile

Some people desire to reconnect with estranged family members and repair the relationship to move forward together. Reconciliation can indeed happen, but can be impossible. Keep in mind that you can choose your own actions and responses, but it's out of your control how others will react.

These tips can't guarantee a positive outcome, but they can make the process go more smoothly and contribute to success:

**Make sure everyone is willing to attempt reconciliation:** Trying to force someone who isn't ready into talking about solutions is likely to end in a further rift. Avoid forcing someone to talk or being forced into talking.

**Know your reason for reconciliation:** Having a specific purpose can help motivate you and make your communication targeted toward a goal. This also helps you avoid being driven by emotions such as nostalgia and temporary desires sparked by events such as holidays or family traditions.

**Have conversations on neutral territory:** This way, neither party has an advantage or risk of being emotionally triggered by the location. You may consider having conversations only with a mediator or therapist present to help with heated conflicts.

**Be emotionally prepared:** Talks may become heated. Make sure you can remain calm and neutral, which a therapist can help with.

**Accept and respect each other despite differences:** Each person has a unique perspective on the situation. Agree ahead of time to respect each other's experiences as valid even if you don't share the same interpretations. Accept each other as unique individuals and listen to each other fully without becoming defensive.

**Be willing to acknowledge your own contribution to the problem and apologize:** In most cases of estrangement, everyone has some degree of responsibility for things that have gone wrong. Even if your own part is small, be willing to admit to your contribution and offer a sincere apology.

**Seek professional help:** Working with a therapist, either individually or together, can go a long way toward peaceful reconciliation. This is especially important when emotions are strong and acceptance and apologies are difficult.

## Therapy and Coping With Estrangement

Estrangement can be traumatic and extremely difficult to deal with on your own. Professional mental health therapy can help you cope with the negative impact of estrangement. Working with a therapist, either individually or in group therapy, can be very healing and empowering because it can help you process difficult feelings that you may have had for a long time. Further, it can help you rebuild trust in others in your life as you create and work toward stronger, healthy relationships in general.

Therapy can also help your family work toward reconciliation, if you so desire. Family therapy, including approaches such as strategic family therapy and structural family therapy, can be extremely beneficial in re-establishing healthy communication and setting and working toward common goals.

Choosing the right therapist is an important part of the process because working with someone you trust and who you feel listens to you deeply contributes to success. An online directory is a great place to find a therapist to help you work through estrangement.

## Statistics on Family Estrangement

These statistics help tell the tale of estrangement. They show that, if you are estranged from one or more family members, you are not alone. They also paint a picture of how long estrangement sometimes lasts and how people feel about reconciliation.

## Who Is Affected by Estrangement

Estrangement isn't a rare situation experienced by just a handful of people. It is surprisingly common, perhaps as common as divorce, and can occur in any family:

- Approximately 12% of adults are estranged from their grown children.
- In a survey of young adults, about 17% indicated that they were estranged from at least one parent, usually their father.
- Sibling estrangement isn't as common as parent-child estrangement, but it does occur. About 5% of Americans report being estranged from one or more siblings.
- In a random sampling of over 550 mothers, 10% indicated estrangement from at least one child.
- In the United Kingdom, about 20% of people report experiencing family estrangement.

A 2015 online survey of estranged individuals with 807 participants, conducted in collaboration between the

University of Cambridge and the non-profit organization StandAlone revealed the following:

- 53% were estranged from their mother (biological or otherwise)
- 43% were estranged from their father (biological or otherwise)
- 34% were estranged from both parents
- 44% were estranged from one or more sisters
- 44% were estranged from one or more brothers
- 14% were estranged from both brothers and sisters
- 80% indicated that being estranged brought positive outcomes like greater independence

## How Long Estrangement Lasts

Estrangement varies greatly in length. For some, it can be fairly brief while for other families the rift is permanent. Recall that estrangement is often a process involving periods of complete distancing and periods of reconciliation. This pattern makes the length of estrangement difficult to measure and highly variable.

Still, some surveys have shed light on how long estrangement can last:

- In a survey of 354 undergraduate and graduate students, ages 18-56, from four universities in the northeastern United States, 43% reported having experienced estrangement from their nuclear families, and most lasted fewer than four years.
- A different survey revealed that the average length of parent-child estrangement is nine years.
- Estrangement from fathers has been reported to last longer than estrangement from mothers, with the length more than five years from mothers and more than seven years from fathers.

**Estrangement Reconciliation**

As with length of estrangement, rate of reconciliation is difficult to accurately measure because there are so many individual differences and unique circumstances which are complicated by the tendency of many families to cycle in periods of separation and reconciliation.

Some surveys have attempted to determine how common reconciliation is once family members become estranged from one another:

- Almost 80% of estranged individuals believe that reconciliation is impossible.
- In a survey, approximately 71% of children who cut ties with parents do end up reconciling.
- The same survey indicated that approximately 30% of estranged parents and children remain distanced.
- A different survey indicated that 46% of estranged families ended up reconciling.

Hence, family estrangement can be difficult and negatively affect your mental health and wellbeing. It doesn't have to be permanent, and there are ways to reconcile, if you so desire. Working with a therapist can be highly valuable in either helping you reconcile or cope positively with long-term estrangement.

# CHAPTER 2

# Family Estrangement

Family estrangement happens when contact is cut off between family members. It can last for long periods of time or go through cycles where there is intermittent communication and reconciliation. Often, apathy or antagonism are the driving factors for the distance. Family estrangement can occur between parents and children, siblings, or other relatives.

## Signs of Family Estrangement

There are several factors that create estrangement between family members. A 2017 study of 52 adult children who were separating from their parents noted eight main factors in their estrangement.

18

## Communication Quantity and Quality

Two signs of estrangement involve communication quantity and quality. A lack of communication could look like a complete lack of contact; frequently but not always ignoring a family member's attempts to reach you; or solely communicating through a third party. If and when you do touch base with your estranged family member, you avoid discussing topics that are significant to your life.

## Physical Distance

Estrangement can also be facilitated by intentionally putting physical distance between yourself and a family member. Maybe one of you moved out of a previously shared home, or you decided to move to another place on the map entirely. You may no longer share holidays or major events.

## Presence/Absence of Emotion

There is a wide range of emotions involved in estrangement. Stand Alone, a United Kingdom-based charity supporting people who are estranged, notes that one day you may feel lonely and another relieved to have cut contact. At the same time, you might start to lack a feeling of any connection at all to the person from whom you are estranged.

## Positive/Negative Affect

For some adult children estranged from their parents, there is not only an absence of positive sentiment but also extreme negative feelings of dislike.

## Reconciliation and the Desire to Be a Family

A willingness or refusal to reconcile is a polarizing part of estrangement. Some families have a desire to reconnect. Others have accepted their separation as permanent.

## Role Reciprocity

When a parent-child relationship differs from what you traditionally expect, it can leave you feeling like your needs are not being met and lead to distance.

**Taking Legal Action**

Estrangement is also present in certain legal proceedings, such as the emancipation of a child or a transfer of the power of attorney.

## Causes of Family Estrangement

Why do relationships between adult children and their parents break down? It depends on which group you ask.

In 2015, more than 800 people contributed to a report titled "Hidden Voices: Family Estrangement in Adulthood," a joint product of the Centre for Family Research at the University of Cambridge (U.K.) and Stand Alone.

The group participating was about half British, with the remainder coming from the United States and other countries. It was diversified in indicators such as age, marital status, religious affiliation, and level of education. The respondents were, however, 89% female and 88% white.

The survey found that adult children estranged from their parents reported four issues that affected their relationships:

- Clashes based on personalities or value systems
- Differing expectations about family roles
- Emotional abuse
- Neglect

Parents estranged from their children cited three causes that were common to both sons and daughters:

- Differing expectations about family roles
- divorce-related issues
- a traumatic event

## Impact of Family Estrangement

Family members who are estranged have varying experiences. Some may feel free or at peace, while others may feel isolated and aggravated. These emotions can be fleeting or persistent. Therapy could be a beneficial route for those who are struggling with estrangement.

Holidays can be particularly challenging if you no longer have a place to celebrate or are experiencing the absence of a family member. Estrangement can affect your social life. For example, you may be uncomfortable talking about your family life with friends or co-workers. Another person's mention of children or grandchildren could stir up memories or difficult feelings.

## Statistics on Family Estrangement

The 2015 "Hidden Voices" study provided various statistics to paint a view of family estrangement. It cited 455 participants as estranged from a mother and 350 as estranged from a father. Participants who were estranged from both totaled 277.

Additionally, "Hidden Voices" noted 152 people were estranged from a daughter and 138 were estranged from one or more sons. There were 361 participants estranged from one or more sisters and 362 people estranged from one or more brothers.

Another 2015 study, "Family Estrangement: Establishing a Prevalence Rate," noted that out of its 154 participants,

43.5% experienced estrangement. Of the people involved, the study cited 14.8% as estranged from their grandfather and 3.7% as estranged from their grandmother.

**Gender Differences**

In "Hidden Voices," more respondents reported being estranged from mothers than from fathers or from both parents. More parents reported being estranged from daughters than from sons. Interestingly, however, estrangement from male family members tended to be longer-lasting than estrangement from female family members.

People estranged from their mothers also cited mental health problems, while those estranged from fathers more often cited a traumatic family event.

Parents estranged from daughters also reported mental health problems and emotional abuse, whereas those estranged from sons reported issues relating to marriage and in-laws.

Among the more than 800 participants in the "Hidden Voices" report, estrangement from fathers averaged 7.9 years, whereas estrangement from mothers averaged 5.5 years. Parents reported estrangements from sons lasting an average of 5.2 years versus 3.8 years for daughters.

Relationship breakdowns were more likely to be intermittent with female relatives than with male relatives. When participants were asked about relationships in which they cycled in and out of estrangement, only 29% of those reporting on relationships with mothers said there had been no cycles, meaning an unbroken history of estrangement, while 21% reported five or more cycles.

For those reporting on relationships with fathers, 36% reported no cycles and only 16% said there had been five or more cycles. A similar pattern was observed with daughters and sons.

Among those reporting estrangement from daughters, 37% reported no cycling in and out of the relationship. On the other extreme, 20% reported five or more cycles.

Among those reporting estrangement from sons, 41% reported no cycles and only 11% reported five or more cycles.

**Effects of Gender Differences**

The "Hidden Voices" findings are consistent with research about woman-to-woman conflict. Of course, there are individual differences that are involved with estrangement but the possibility of gender variations may be related to conflict-resolution styles.

In a conflict, males tend to employ a "fight or flight" strategy, and family conflict often results in the "flight" option, meaning that males often withdraw from the conflict. Because men may refuse to engage, the estrangement tends to be long-lasting and intractable.

Women under pressure, on the other hand, may more often have a "tend and befriend" pattern. They may deal with stress by seeking closeness with others. So if they forsake a relationship with a relative, they may feel a lot of pressure to re-establish the relationship.

## Differences Between Generations

Adult children are more likely to initiate a break of contact with their parents and be less open to reconciliation. The "Hidden Voices" study shared that 50% of children estranged from a parent say that they cut off contact. Only 5% to 6% of those estranged from a son or daughter say that they made the move.

## Views of Parents vs. Children

"Family Estrangement" studied the different reasons why parents may cut off from their children and vice versa. It reported that parents stopped communicating with their children because of relationships outside of the family as well as situational or family stressors. For children, a parent's lack of support, toxic behavior, or inability to accept them were the main reasons for estrangement.

When discussing generational differences in reasons for estrangement, it's also worth exploring the concept of family circles.

Parents' bonds with their children are commonly the strongest familial bonds they form, and many times, parental bonds prove to be stronger than attachments to partners or spouses. Children, on the other hand, while likely to have strong bonds with their parents, may themselves become parents, and their bonds with their children may supplant those with their own parents.

For many parents, their children are in their primary circle. But when adult children have children of their own, their parents may be relegated to a secondary circle. In a sense, the parent's loss is objectively greater. Estrangement from adult children usually means a loss of contact with grandchildren, too. Alienation from grandchildren brings its own emotional toll.

## What You Can Do

According to the research, adult children may often find it more difficult or impossible to reconcile with their parents, but they are still usually willing to give their parents another chance. It's up to estranged parents, who are commonly more open to reconciliation, to make those chances count.

When questioned about what they wanted from their parents in the "Hidden Voices" study, adult children said they wanted relationships that are:

- Closer
- More positive
- More loving

In addition, adult children wished their mothers would be less critical and judgmental; they wanted their mothers to acknowledge when they have engaged in hurtful behavior. Adult children also wished that their fathers would take more interest in their lives. They wanted them to stand up to other family members, including their spouses or partners.

If you'd like to try to move forward in your relationships, keep these tips in mind.

- Parents/grandparents should try to provide emotional support, reduce drama, and be less critical.
- Parents should strive to get along with their child's partner and also with their in-laws.

So, whether by choice or by circumstance, family estrangement can be complex and painful. It can also be isolating, as it may be hard for others to understand. Whether the steps forward include learning to live without that familial connection or seeking to reconcile, individual or family therapy can be helpful to sort out difficult feelings related to relationships with your family members.

# CHAPTER 3

# Causes & How To Deal With Family Estrangement

It's painful and isolating to be apart from your family. Family estrangement is a difficult thing to deal with.

In a nuclear family, parent-child relationships are some of the most long-lasting and close relationships one experiences. However, not all parent-child communication is positive. When family members choose to withdraw from one another, it can be upsetting.

Sometimes, it's hard to understand why a family member would want to cut another member out of their life.

Family estrangement is a separation within a family, often involving one or more members of the family choosing to withdraw from one another. It often happens between adult children and their parents, but estrangements between parents also exist.

Cutting off contact and communication is one of the most common ways people use to distance themselves from the family or certain family members.

There are two types of family rifts:

- continuous estrangement
- chaotic disassociation.

A continuous estrangement happens when adult children are able to communicate effectively with their parents and maintain distance from them in spite of social or cultural pressures to reconcile.

In chaotic disassociation, adult children succumb to pressure and engage in an on-and-off relationship until they can finally cut off all family ties.

## How Common Is Family Estrangement

A 1997 study on later-life intergenerational relationships shows that 7% of adults children are estranged from mothers and 27% from fathers. In 2015, a survey conducted with 354 undergraduate and graduate students at universities in the northeastern US found that 44% experienced an estrangement.

## What Causes Family Estrangement?

There are many reasons why people may experience or instigate estrangement from their families. Often, estrangement occurs after a major event or incident, but the event usually serves as a trigger rather than the main cause.

Studies show that there is no one type of interaction, one parenting style, or one significant family conflict that leads to estrangement. However, one common theme researchers have noticed is that parents' and children's reasons for estrangement differ significantly from each other.

While parents reported their primary reason for becoming estranged stemmed from their own divorce, their children's objectionable relationships or their sense of entitlement, adult children most frequently attributed their estrangement to their parents' toxic behavior, maltreatment, child abuse, neglect or feeling unsupported and/or unaccepted.

Additionally, a higher proportion of estranged parents than estranged children do not know exactly why they are estranged, which means children are more likely to initiate estrangement than parents.

A large study involving 898 estranged parent-child pairs discovered that there are three categories of reasons why adult children seek distance from their parents:

**Intrapersonal Issues – Personality Characteristic of The Involved Members**

- mental illness
- self-centeredness, narcissism
- unsupported or unaccepted feelings or judgment
- immaturity

- differences in personal values such as sexual orientation, religious belief

**Intrafamily Issues – Resulted from Negative Behavior Between Estranged Family Members**

- abuse in childhood, including physical abuse, sexual abuse, emotional abuse, abuse by siblings
- serious neglect or insensitivities
- rigid, controlling or harsh parenting
- distant parenting style
- family conflict or rivalry
- existence or perception of parental favoritism
- lying or manipulation
- ambivalent about parent-child relationship
- entitlement
- drug or alcohol abuse
- alienation – child's relationship with a parent is undermined or damaged by input from the alienating parent in intense marital conflicts
- enmeshment – enmeshed relationship between the child and the preferred parent

- toxic behavior
- difficulties in managing anger and disappointment
- violation of societal norm such as crime, incarceration

## Interfamily Issues – Issues Outside of The Family

- objectional relationship
- physical distance
- influence from third party, such as a controlling or abusive spouse

## The Effects of Family Estrangement

The effects of estrangement between family members can be devastating to some members. It may create substantial distress for the estranged individuals.

A general belief in society is that relationships between parents and children are deeply meaningful, lifelong and highly rewarding. The adage "blood is thicker than water" is deeply ingrained in American family values. Despite whatever hardship, many believe that family relationship bound by blood can survive insurmountable odds. Therefore, any breach of that closeness is discouraged.

On one hand, the involuntary nature of family relationships coupled with their 'staying power' creates great distress for those who struggle to understand why estrangement has happened. On the other hand, individuals who believe they have no viable choice but to maintain such relationships will be greatly distressed.

For an abuse survivor, breaking the rules of family life and estranging from the abusive family is necessary to obtain a better quality of life. Recent "individualistic culture" has afforded these people the courage to break free from harm.

In other cases, for family estrangement to occur, communication must break down or the family situation must be so intolerable that those initiating the separation feel the need to end the difficult relationship to protect their own mental health. When this happens, the rejected parent often experiences the difficult feelings of loss, abandonment, rejection, and helplessness.

For some adult children, their social network or extended family members may pressure them constantly to reconcile, which results in a cycle of on-again/off-again relationship and estranged family tension. However, chronic stress caused by toxic parenting can lead to a range of physical and mental health problems for the adult children. A vast majority of adult children make this decision to improve the quality of their adult lives.

**How To Deal With Estrangement From Your Children**

In studies, although grief of family estrangement created profound feelings in parents, they often cited intra- and interfamily stressors significantly more than children. These parents believe that situational or external stressors play a greater role than their children's character or personality in creating the rupture. That means, if those external circumstances are absent, the broken family ties would likely be repaired.

If you believe this is the case in your situation, it is a relatively easier problem to fix because you don't have to change your child. All you have to do is to provide them with new information or experiences.

However, if you are estranged from your adult children due to intrapersonal reasons, e.g. your personality or differences in values, then estrangement may be inevitable unless significant changes can occur in you or your child.

It is hard for any person to identify and accept their own flaws. When asked by researchers in the study, parents often cannot reflect on their own roles in creating hurtful feelings in their children.

Therefore, to overcome the estrangement and get your relationship back on track, it is advisable to seek help from family counselling, family therapist or other mental health professional. They will likely have a different perspective on the situation.

Asking your children for their honest feedback is another way. But keep in mind that the truth may hurt and may change the family dynamic in unexcepted ways.

# CHAPTER 4

# 'Divorce' Between Adult Children and Parents

Papers aren't filed, and no judge hears the case, but more and more adult children are divorcing their parents, often completely cutting off contact. What's driving the increase in parent-child estrangement? Professionals who work with families have some ideas, and thousands of individuals have shared their experiences in surveys. Definitive answers may be elusive, but it's fairly easy to get a feel for some of the issues.

## Statistics on Estrangement

Both parents and adult children can fill out surveys about their estrangement. The results can be surprising. The parents who are estranged are older than one might expect, with over one-third falling into the 70- to 80-year-old age group.

When asked to describe the parent-child relationship before the rift, the most popular answer given by the adult children was that they maintained it out of "moral obligation." The second most popular answer was to describe the relationship as "volatile and/or not close." When asked whether they bear some responsibility for the estrangement, slightly more than half said yes.

Another interesting area concerns whether the children ever told the cut-off parent the reasons for the estrangement. Over 67% said they had. This is a reverse mirror image of the parents' response in a similar survey when over 60% said that they had never been told the reasons for the estrangement. This disparity reflects difficulties that parents sometimes have in communicating with adult children.

A British survey found that children are usually the ones who cut off contact. When parents were asked about the estrangement, nearly three-quarters said their daughter (74.5%) or son (73%) had initiated the break.

When children were asked about their estrangement from parents, their answers were similar. Among those estranged from mothers, 55% said they initiated the break and 10% said their mother cut them off. Children estranged from their fathers initiated the break 51% of the time and were cut off 14% of the time.

**Reasons for Estrangement**

Reasons for conflicts between parents and adult children vary. Some adult children have severed relationships with parents due to traumatic childhoods: They were abused or grew up with parents whose drug or alcohol addictions interfered with their parenting.

Occasionally, family disputes have erupted over money. In the majority of cases, however, the reasons for estrangement are not so clear-cut. Still, certain themes occur over and over in commentary from adult children who have divorced their parents.

## "You Weren't a Good Parent"

Some children feel that they weren't loved or nurtured sufficiently. Sometimes that is because they were reared in a time or a culture that didn't value open expressions of love. Sometimes it is because their parents truly had a hard time expressing their feelings. Occasionally adult children still feel hurt from episodes that occurred years ago, episodes that the parents may not even be aware of.

## "You Still See Me as a Child"

Parents and children live for many years in a specific relationship, with parents in charge. Parents sometimes have difficulty giving up that construct. When adult children say that their parents don't see them as adults, they are sometimes correct. Many times parents persist in giving unwanted advice. Voicing disapproval of a child's spouse, finances, job, or lifestyle can definitely cause conflict.

## "We Don't Have the Same Values"

When children make choices that aren't consistent with their parents' values, the parents sometimes say, "We didn't raise you that way." They have trouble acknowledging that grown children are responsible for developing their own moral compasses.

Trouble can also arise when an adult child marries someone who differs in important ways from their family of birth. Sometimes the difficulty springs from differences in political leanings or religious beliefs. These issues present especially difficult challenges because such beliefs tend to be closely held. Some families learn to live with differences. Others never do.

## "You're a Toxic Person"

Exactly what is meant by a "toxic" person depends upon the speaker. Generally, it's understood to mean a person who is harmful to another's emotional equilibrium. Those who are overwhelmingly negative, blame others, are excessively needy, or are casually cruel sometimes are called toxic.

Other labels that are often used to justify ending a relationship are "narcissistic" and "bipolar." Both of these refer to genuine psychological disorders, but the labels are often casually applied, without any professional diagnosis.

## Does Divorce Contribute to Estrangement?

Many parents blame their own divorce for their estrangement from adult children. Among those estranged from daughters, 50% said a divorce was a "very relevant" factor, compared to 37% of parents estranged from sons. Some believe their children blame them for not trying harder to keep the family together. Others feel that their ex-partner pitted their child against them through persuasion or manipulation.

However, multiple studies suggest that most adult children don't see divorce as a major factor in their estrangement. Instead, the younger generation typically attributes the separation due to the parent's own behaviors, such as neglect or criticism.

Every family has its own unique circumstances. In some cases, it is possible that children were manipulated into seeing the estranged parent's behavior as problematic. In other cases, the estranged parents may have coped poorly with divorce and blamed third-party interference rather than their own actions. How a divorce influences the parent-child relationship depends on the individuals involved.

## The Possibility of Reconciliation

Overwhelmingly, adult children who have divorced their parents say that they did it for the good of their families, or for their own good. When asked whether the parents should try for reconciliation, answers vary. Some consider any attempt at communication as harassment.

In the Estranged Stories survey, however, around 60% of adult children said that they would like to have a relationship with the person from whom they were estranged. The steps cited most often that could affect a reconciliation were apologies from parents, parents taking responsibility, and boundary setting.

In the British study, Hidden Voices, adult children were much more likely than the parents to say that the situation was hopeless, with no chance of reconciliation. In fact, over 70% agreed or strongly agreed with the notion that having a functional relationship with their mother or father in the future was not a possibility.

Still, parents in this situation should not give up hope. Young people have been known to change their minds as they get older and gain life experience. And parents can draw encouragement from the knowledge that even if they have been divorced, the decree is not final.

# CHAPTER 5

# Reasons Why Adult Children Cut off Their Parents

Children cut off their parents for a variety of reasons, and it can be difficult to understand why if you feel like this was done without warning, or in your opinion, justification. In many cases of cutoff, the parent or parents are completely unaware as to why this happened. It's really important to be open to understanding your child's reasoning if you want to have a healthy reconciliation and work towards improving your relationship. This means instead of blaming them, trying to understand their unique perspective without judgment. Some common reasons for cutoff include:

48

- Unhealthy attachment pattern with one or both parents - these are very likely in these circumstances and can feel like the invisible barrier between you and your daughter
- Verbal abuse, physical abuse, manipulation, and/or emotional abuse
- Instilling in her that you are correct and her instincts are wrong
- Teaching her she can't trust herself (belittling her opinion, telling her she's wrong often, pointing out her faults often)
- Forcing a rigid self image and/or belief system on her that she doesn't subscribe to
- Parentifying her throughout her childhood (asking her to emotionally take care of you, which you may have done unconsciously based on your own history of family or origin patterns)

As a parent, it's your job to love your child unconditionally and provide a safe, loving, and nurturing environment for them to thrive and become the person they want to be. If your daughter feels otherwise, it's critical that you take the time to understand her perspective so you can work on boosting the health of your relationship. Remember that even if you feel you provided a safe space for her, if she doesn't, that's what matters and it's up to you to self-reflect and understand her perspective.

**How Do I Reconnect With My Daughter?**

Reconnecting with your daughter after being cutoff can be an incredibly intense emotional process. If you feel defensive or emotionally unprepared to connect with her in healthy ways, it's critical to reach out to a therapist who can help you develop insight. Doing so may not only help you improve your own mental health, but increases your chances of being able to connect with her in an emotionally safer way if she agrees to communicate with you.

## Conflicts That Can Lead to Grandparent Estrangement

When grandparents are unfairly denied contact with their grandchildren, it can be heartbreaking for the grandparents and grandchildren alike. Although suing for visitation rights is a possibility, the most productive approach is resolving family disputes before estrangement is on the table.

Family members have a responsibility to navigate disputes and disagreements before they become an issue. Here is an overview of the most common disputes among parents and grandparents that can lead to withholding contact with grandchildren.

**Deal-Breaking Behavior**

Sometimes parents are right to deny grandparents contact with grandchildren. People who are sex offenders or substance abusers seldom clean up their acts just because they become grandparents. Parents are justified in not wanting their children around grandparents who could endanger children's welfare.

Parents also are justified in denying contact to grandparents who disregard the parents' rules about safety.

For instance, grandparents who transport grandchildren without using the proper car safety restraints, have a history or accidents, or do not drive safely should not be allowed to drive grandchildren anywhere. The same goes for any other safety rule established by the parents, whether the grandparents agree with it or not.

If the infringement is not too great, parents might consider allowing the grandparents to see the grandchildren, but only under controlled conditions. Other actions by grandparents that can easily trigger a family dispute include the following:

- Undermining parental authority: Encouraging children to disobey parents, or forgetting how hard parenting can be
- Speaking ill of family members, including parents, stepparents, or other grandparents
- Refusing to follow parents' rules: Disregarding guidelines for diet, screen time, bedtimes, and so on

- Giving grandchildren questionable gifts, especially gifts that parents would not approve of
- Pressuring parents for more contact, such as overnight visits, when parents are reluctant

Families should be able to resolve less serious matters without cutting off contact between grandparents and grandchildren. The ideal approach is to discuss boundaries and behavior and talk about issues as soon as they crop up.

## Threats to Normal Access

Barring grandparent misconduct, the expectation of the law is that grandparents have access to their grandchildren through the parent who is their child. This is expected to be true both in intact families and in cases where the child's parents are no longer together.

Sometimes, however, the parent who serves as the grandparent's portal to grandchildren also loses contact with the children. This situation can occur for a number of reasons, the most devastating, of course, being the death of the parent. Other complicating situations include:

- The parents are unmarried and the noncustodial parent has not secured their parental rights.
- A parent has given up their parental rights.
- A parent is incarcerated.
- A parent is barred from seeing the child due to substance abuse, a sexual offense, domestic violence, or something similar.
- The parent with custody moves a long distance away from the grandparents.
- The parent who would normally supply access to the grandchildren moves a long distance away.

Another common situation that causes grandparents to be cut off from their grandchildren occurs when the parents struggle with addiction. Parents who misuse drugs or alcohol and deal with addiction often want to keep their habits secret.

If an addiction becomes so severe that it is hard to hide, parents may break contact with the grandparents. The primary motivation is to keep their addiction from being exposed. Such family ruptures can be very ugly and can put grandparents in the unenviable position of suing for visitation rights to try to help their grandchildren.

## Generational Disputes

There are other, less serious conflicts that also can lead to family estrangement. According to psychologist Marsha L. Shelov, three common circumstances that spark disputes between parents and grandparents include:

- Disagreements over issues such as religion
- Personality conflicts between grandparents and parents, such as daughter-in-law conflicts
- Old parent-child conflicts that continue to affect the relationship

These three issues can cause serious family disputes. But, they also can be alleviated if grandparents are extra conciliatory and accommodating.

As difficult as that can be, especially for grandparents who believe that they are right, giving a little is infinitely preferable to losing contact with grandchildren. If the family conflict is especially bitter or involves unresolved issues, family counseling can be helpful as well.

**Financial Issues**

Sometimes family disputes concern money. For instance, grandparents who contribute financially to their children sometimes threaten to cut off financial aid unless certain conditions are met.

Ideally, grandparents who choose to give financial assistance should give it freely and refrain from using money as a means of control—or else they should reconsider the gift.

The exception to this rule is when grandparents agree to pay for private school, college, special lessons, or coaching for their grandchildren. In these circumstances, they have a right to require that their contributions be used as designated.

On the other hand, parents also may use money as a means of control. For instance, they may threaten to withhold contact with the grandchildren unless financial demands are met.

Additionally, parents who have received loans from grandparents may cut off contact to reduce the pressure of repaying the loans. Before making any monetary transactions, both parents and grandparents should consider what types of conflicts they may create down the road.

**Conflicts and Mental Disorders**

Unfortunately, it is not uncommon for both parents and grandparents to sometimes describe the other parties as mentally ill. Common charges are that the other party is a compulsive liar or has a serious mental illness such as bipolar disorder or narcissistic personality disorder.

Sometimes the individuals in question have been diagnosed with a mental illness, and sometimes someone is playing amateur psychiatrist. If a parent or grandparent is truly mentally ill, every effort should be made to obtain help.

On the other hand, leveling such charges against someone just because of a disagreement is both slanderous and counter-productive. It is much better to concentrate on conflict resolution.

**Breaching Boundaries**

Another common reason why parents restrict contact with the grandchildren is caused by boundaries. This type of offense can take the form of violating physical boundaries, such as dropping in on family members and entering without knocking.

It also could include trying to take over parental roles or trying to make decisions for the family like taking away the baby's pacifier.

Sometimes, the boundaries between parenting and grandparenting are blurred. This situation is often seen when young parents need help and grandparents assume parenting roles. Sometimes the grandparents even assume custody; but more commonly they simply provide child care and often financial assistance.

Then, when the parents decide to reclaim their parenting roles, grandparents sometimes have trouble relinquishing them. Often, the result is that grandparents who have been extremely close to their grandchildren are cut off from them because the parents are desperate to reclaim their parenting turf.

Wise grandparents avoid such rifts by asking for patience as they make the transition. They also do what they can to help the parent resume their responsibilities while relishing the opportunity to enjoy their grandchildren as grandparents rather than bearing the many responsibilities of the parental role.

So, the key to any healthy relationship is effective communication. Many family disagreements are the result of miscommunication and hurt feelings.

Healing small disagreements and family rifts before they become full-blown breaks is the key to maintaining a positive relationship and maintaining contact with your grandchildren. Be the first to apologize and look for a compromise rather than trying to prove a point.

By doing so, you will help ensure you have a regular presence in your grandchildren's lives and a peaceful relationship with their parents.

# CHAPTER 6

# Things Your Estranged Child Wants You To Do

Mistakes estranged parents make that ensure there will be no reconciliation

I know that every parent of an estranged child dreams of reconciliation. It is the thing that we want more than life itself. But many parents are continuing to make mistakes that may prevent that from ever happening. I know, because I have been guilty of this.

I know everyone is at a different place in their journey of estrangement. I have been on this journey for a long time and I have made all the mistakes there are to make. Finally, I have arrived at the place where I am willing to see myself without blinders on. You may not be there yet, and that's ok.

Sometimes it is hard to see ourselves until someone holds a mirror up for us. I have been lucky enough to have people who have been ruthless in their attempts to make me see myself clearly — mostly estranged adult children who have responded to my stories. While this has been painful, it has enabled me to (hopefully) move closer to a real possibility of reconciliation. I hope the things I have learned from estranged adult children will help you, too.

It is not my intent to shame anyone, but to simply offer what I have learned. It is painful to see the truth about ourselves, and if you are not in a place that this is possible, or you feel that this chapter is not for you, you have my blessing to stop reading.

I know there are as many reasons why a child estranges themselves from a parent as there are children who do. Maybe your child has mental health issues or poor coping strategies. Maybe you are truly innocent in the estrangement. I know that is possible. And if that is the case, I may not be talking to you. Sometimes things go wrong that are not our fault at all. Many times adult children estrange themselves because they don't have the emotional skills to express their own pain. All these things can happen without the parents being culpable. But I also know that sometimes, there are things parents do, innocently enough, that contribute to the break in the relationship.

Please take what you can from my own experiences and leave the rest. From one parent to another, I see your pain and it is not my intent to add to it. My wish is for you to find peace and, if possible, reconciliation.

The following are the things that I have heard many estranged adult children say they wish their parents would do. These thoughts did not originate with me. I have simply fleshed out the responses I have received from my stories— they are the words of children who have made the painful decision to walk away from their parents.

**Stop Defending Yourself**

When we are in defense mode, we are unable to see the other person's point of view. You may think that you never did anything wrong, but you need to be open to the possibility. After all, you are human. We all are. You make mistakes because you have your own misguided ideas about how things should be, who your children should be and what your role as a parent is. The point is, you have to be willing to admit you made a mistake if you hope to heal the relationship.

Many parents say their child had no reason to walk away. They (the parents) did nothing wrong. They were good parents. I think I'm a good parent, too. But even good parents can make mistakes and we need to get curious about where we might have veered off the path. It doesn't mean we are horrible people. But until we are ready to drop the shield of defense and see our part in the estrangement, even though it's very painful, we can all but guarantee that the door will never open for us to reconcile.

## Get Really Honest with Yourself

There are a lot of ways that parents of estranged children are not honest with themselves. We create our own stories about what we think happened, and many times it does not include any mistakes that we feel were bad enough to warrant the estrangement. It is too painful for many of us to see that we actually did hurt our child.

I was certainly guilty of this. Because we always did our best, and never intended to harm our children, we don't want to see the ways we did. It takes a great deal of courage to pull the curtain back and see the wizard in all his frail humanity operating the smoke and mirrors. When I did, I could see that I have lied to myself all these years.

I now see the ways I abandoned my daughter at a very critical time of her life, even though at the time I would not have called it abandonment. I was always there, but not always in the way she needed me to be or at the times she needed me. I see that now. Seeing the ways I hurt my daughter is painful, but it was an essential step toward my own growth and toward a possible reconciliation.

## Don't Justify Yourself and Call it an Apology

You may be tempted to start your apology with "I'm sorry for whatever it is you think I did wrong, but I always did my best."

Please don't do this. How would you respond to an apology like that?

I remember when someone blew her cool with me, screaming red-faced at me for something I was not guilty of. Later, when she decided to apologize, she said "I'm sorry, but if you had told me xyz first I wouldn't have yelled at you."

Can you see the twist in that apology that made it my fault she lost it? It was not an apology at all. It was a justification of her behavior.

If you ever hope to reconcile with your child, your apology must be a true apology. If you have done some soul searching and have seen some of the ways you failed, start there. Say something like this:

*"I am so sorry for the ways I abandoned you after the divorce. I know that you must have felt unsafe and I can only imagine how painful that was for you. It was always my intent to keep you safe. I am sorry that I failed in that intention."*

If you truly can't come up with anything you did that might have hurt your child, then this is what you should say if you hope to ever start a conversation that will lead to reconciliation.

*"I know that I have hurt you. I am open to hearing about your experience so I can better understand how I caused you pain."*

That's it. Do not justify yourself. There are a lot of reasons parents fail their children. I have my own reasons. But that does not make their pain go away. If we are unwilling to take responsibility for what we have done, we may never have the opportunity to have that conversation. Our reasons should not be a part of the conversation.

## Don't Make Your Child Responsible for your Happiness

Saying things like *"You have hurt me so much I just want to die"* or *"How could you walk away from me like this, I am your mother!"* will not bring them back into your loving arms.

If you think your children came into the world just to meet your emotional needs, you need to go back to the beginning and think that through. We bring our children into the world to find their way and make lives for themselves. We happen to be parents whose children chose to do that without us along for the trip. It really sucks, I know. But what sucks more is expecting someone else to make us happy.

Saying we deserve their respect, no matter what, is a sign that we are clueless about how to have a healthy relationship with them. Our children really don't owe us anything. We gave them all that we gave them because we love them, not to make them beholden to us. At least that is how I understand parental love. I chose to give my daughter all the love and support and material things I gave without any strings attached. When we attach strings, it is no longer love, it is hostage- taking.

Never, ever say to your child, "After all I did for you, you treat me like this?"

## Stop Playing the Victim

Your child has walked out of your life. This is the hardest thing you have probably ever had to face. But you are not a victim unless you make yourself one.

When we adopt a victim mentality, we refuse to take responsibility for our life and happiness. We are always pointing the finger at someone else who is responsible for our misery. We don't take the steps to improve our life because we believe that we can't change until someone else changes. We rehearse our story over and over again, always attempting to find sympathy for our plight.

While we all fall into these behaviors sometimes, the goal should be to break free from these counterproductive ways of thinking and get on with building your life. If our children are to ever come back, they need a parent who is busy living a life, not one who is drowning in self-pity.

John Wooden says, "You can make mistakes, but you aren't a failure until you start blaming others for those mistakes."

## Do Not Ask Family Members to take Sides

One of the hardest things to do is see your child carrying on relationships with other people in the family. But one of the most selfless things you can do is not try to make others choose. If you really love your child as you say you do, you will step back from trying to influence others. This is between you and your child, and unless you are intent on making this thing bigger than it is, leave it alone.

My daughter still has a close relationship with my mother. In the beginning it was so painful for me to know that she was with my mom, not because I resented her being there, but because I wanted to be there with her, too. But I recognized how beneficial this relationship is for both of them, and I kept my feelings to myself. I sincerely love my daughter, and trying to influence my mother against her would not be loving at all.

Your family is already broken with this estrangement. Don't let yourself be responsible for breaking it any more.

**Fix Yourself, Even if Your Child Never Comes Back**

We may do all the hard work of seeing ourselves clearly, owning our mistakes, and even offer a sincere apology and never get the result we want. We may never have our child in our life again. This is really sad, and really hard, but it is not something you can't overcome.

When we are able to see ourselves as fallible human beings, and learn to offer ourselves compassion for our mistakes, we are then free to move on and live our lives. When those who have done horrible things go on to make restitution for their crimes, they redeem their mistakes for a higher good. Honor your child by doing the same.

Do the work to fix yourself. Staying stuck in your pain and misery does nothing to help others. Even if your child never comes back to see what you have made from your mistakes, the world will benefit. And your child will more likely come back to a parent who is willing to see themselves clearly and is willing to own their failures. It is never a bad idea to do the work.

# CHAPTER 7

# For Parents Who Are Estranged From Adult Children

Hard statistics are hard to come by, but many of those working with families say that they've seen an uptick: More young adults than ever are cutting ties with their parents. For grandparents estranged from their adult children, that often means a loss of contact with their grandchildren as well.

The good news is that many adult children say that they would like to have their parents back in their lives. If you are estranged from your adult child, consider steps you could take to forge a renewed relationship.

## Understand Causes of Estrangement

The causes of conflict with adult children can vary widely as we have discussed in the previous chapters. To reconcile with your child, you will need to be willing to consider their perspective. Sometimes adult children find fault in the way they were reared.

## Authoritarian Parenting Style

Perhaps when your children were growing up, authoritarian parenting was still an acceptable approach to child-rearing. Although parenting began to become more permissive following World War II, it took many years for this change to occur, especially in America's heartland.

Through much of the 20th century, many parents used corporal punishment. In fact, they were told that if they did not use corporal punishment, they were bad parents. Even religious leaders encouraged physical punishment. What many would consider abusive today passed for good old-fashioned parenting not that long ago.

## Lack of Affection

Similarly, adult children sometimes feel that their parents did not nurture them as they should have. In many families of the past, parents seldom expressed affection verbally or physically. The underlying assumption was that parents demonstrated their love for their children by taking care of them. The unfortunate result was that no one worried much about a child's self-esteem.

## Resentments

Adult children sometimes hold on to resentments over their parents' broken marriage, often blaming one partner or another. In other cases, a child's partner is the divisive factor. The parents may not like or approve of the partner. Their disapproval forces the child to choose between parents and partner.

Another common problem is that adult children feel that their parents don't recognize them as adults with the ability to make their own decisions.

## Avoid Defensiveness

Even though It might be possible to justify some of your past actions, becoming defensive is counterproductive. If parents prove that what they did was right or acceptable, then it follows that the other parties (their children) were wrong in their reactions, and proving someone wrong or calling their feelings invalid is not likely to mend any fences.

What adult children say that they crave is for their parents to take responsibility and, in some cases, apologize. State clearly how you feel, if you can do so authentically.

- I'm sorry.
- I understand your feelings.
- I know I made mistakes.
- I could have been more supportive (helpful, understanding, loving, etc.).

## Stay Calm

Parents often want to talk about how much pain the estrangement has caused them. Adult children who have taken the measure of cutting off contact will not be touched by their parents' pain. They are likely to be particularly unmoved by grandparents' grief over not seeing grandchildren.

## Continue the Conversation

It may take more than one overture from a parent before a child agrees to work toward a reconciliation, but the overtures shouldn't feel like harassment. All that is required is a simple proposal to get together for a low-stress occasion such as a dinner or an outing. If the overture is rejected, wait a while and try again.

## If Reconciliation Fails

If attempts to restore the relationship fail, grandparents are in a real bind. Do they give up any hope of seeing their grandchildren?

Sometimes mediation is an effective next step. If mediation fails, or if the other parties are not willing, some grandparents will consider legal action, but there is a lot that grandparents should know before suing for visitation rights. In addition, if the grandchildren live in an intact family, grandparents are unlikely to win visitation in court.

## How to Rekindle a Relationship With Estranged Family Members

Whether you stopped talking to your dad a year ago because he was critical of your identity or partner or values, or you cut your sister out of your life a decade ago because her addiction was out of control, ending a relationship with family members is tough.

Estrangement doesn't always last forever, though. A research project between the UK's University of Cambridge and the non-profit organization, Stand Alone, found that estrangement from fathers was the most common, and that it tends to last an average of almost eight years. Estrangement between brothers tends to last seven and a half years, while between sisters it averages seven years. Estrangement between mothers and their adult children averages five and a half years.

Regardless of how long you've been separated from family, there may come a time when you think about rekindling the relationship. The mere thought of resuming contact might stir up a lot of uncomfortable emotions though—such as fear, sadness, anger, or hurt. But the thought of having a relationship once again might also make you happy at the same time.

When it comes to reconnecting, however, you might not know where to start. How do you reach out? What do you say? And how can you establish a healthy relationship this time?

These strategies can help you make attempts to rekindle the relationship with an estranged family member.

**Determine Intentions**

There are many reasons you might want to resume contact with a family member that you're not in contact with. Before you reconnect, it's important to get clarity on why you want to reconnect and why now is the right time.

## Why You Want to Reconnect

You likely miss that person. You might think about how it will be in the future if you never reconnect. What if one of you passes away before you have a chance to talk?

Your reason for rekindling the relationship might also have less to do with a desire to become close again and more to do with your eagerness to put an end to uncomfortable family gatherings.

Attending a family member's funeral when you are estranged from a relative can be awkward. You might find you skip out on family weddings or events because it's too difficult. You might not even get invited to some events if family members have taken sides.

You might also be pressured by other people to reconnect. Your friends or family members might say things like, "Life is too short to not talk to your mom," or, "Blood runs thicker than water." You may reason that having your family member back in your life just might make life easier.

**Why Now**

When you decide why you want to reconnect—whether for emotional reasons, practical reasons, etc.—think carefully about why you want to reconnect right now.

Has something changed? Perhaps you or the person you're estranged from has changed. Substance abuse treatment or mental health treatment, for example, might have helped them get to the point where you can have a healthy relationship again.

Or one of you might have developed a different outlook at the moment. A parent who once thought your decisions were shameful may have come around to accept you for who you are.

Your situation might also change things. Perhaps you heard the other person was diagnosed with a serious health problem and you want to attempt to reconnect while you can. Or maybe becoming a parent made you rethink things because you want your child to have a relationship with your family.

Get clear on why it's so important for you to connect now and how things have changed since you first became estranged. Doing so will help you move forward with better clarity about your goals.

**Establish Expectations**

Before establishing contact, think about your expectations and the type of relationship you'd like to establish in the future. Here are some questions to consider?

- Do you hope to reconnect in a way that allows you to have a loving, healthy relationship?
- Are you hoping to spend holidays together?
- Do you envision regular, ongoing contact?
- Do you think this person will be available for support? Will you be a support for them?
- Do you expect that you'll be able to communicate any time you want?
- Are you hoping you can attend family functions without things feeling tense?

- Do you hope to have a friendly relationship that doesn't involve a deeper connection?
- Are you looking for the relationship to only involve certain things, such as allowing your children to have contact?

Think about what your hopes are and what you'd expect from yourself and the other person.

## Prepare for All Outcomes

You can control how you reach out to the person, how you present your desire to reconnect, and what you offer to them. But you can't control whether it's well-received.

No matter how good your intentions are, you can't force your estranged family member to rekindle the relationship. And if they choose to ignore your efforts—or they outright refuse to talk—it doesn't necessarily mean you said the wrong thing or reached out in the wrong way. They simply might not be in the same place you are right now.

Before you attempt to rekindle the relationship, you need to know that you're able to handle whatever outcome you face.

This may mean having a support system in place of people who can be there for you if you feel let down, hurt, or rejected. It also might mean having some clear coping skills in place to deal with your emotions—like meditation, exercise, or yoga.

You may also want to consider how you'll deal with the other person's reaction. If they're angry with you, how will you respond? If they try to make you feel guilty, what can you do? Having a plan in place will help you feel equipped and confident as you move forward.

**Make a Plan**

Prepare for reconnecting by making a plan for how it will happen. Determining what to say and how to address past points of pain can help you move into the conversation with confidence.

## Does the Past Need Addressing?

In some situations, the relationship can't be resumed until the past is addressed. Only you and the other person can decide if this is the case.

If you stopped talking to your mother because she dated abusive men during your childhood, you might want to have a conversation about how her choices affected you. Sharing that with her may be important to your healing, and you might think she needs to understand what she put you through before you can have an authentic relationship now.

There may also be times when you decide you need to talk about a situation or issue that led to the estrangement, so you can ensure that it doesn't happen again. For example, if your brother lost his temper and said horrible things to you while under the influence, you might want reassurance that he's gotten treatment for his substance use issues. You also might want to ensure that he doesn't actually think those things he said.

In other instances, you might decide that there's no sense in rehashing the past. Perhaps you and your family member have different values—and that fact hasn't changed. Or maybe you both allowed something to come in between you—like an inheritance—and you know you'll never agree on how the money was divided or spent.

In these types of cases, you might simply decide to focus on the future. Think about how you can have a healthy relationship from here on out.

**Plan What You'll Say**

It can be difficult to know what to say to someone you've been estranged from. The first few words you say can set the tone for the future of your relationship, so it's important to plan your conversation wisely.

Saying something like, "Hi, Mom. I've really missed you," might be a good way to start. The last thing you want to do is dive into an accusation or ask a question that might come across as condescending, such as, "I was just calling to see if you are finally ready to take responsibility for your mistakes."

Ask yourself what would encourage you to stay in the conversation if someone you were estranged from reached out to you first. And try to hold a similar conversation with the other person.

If you are genuinely looking to rekindle the relationship, be kind and proceed slowly. Here are some ways you might start the conversation:

- "I know we haven't had any contact for a long time. But I'd like to change that."
- "I am sure hearing from me is a bit of a surprise, but I'm hoping we can have a conversation."
- "I've missed having you in my life. I'm hoping we can get together for coffee and talk."

Think carefully about how to reach out as well. A phone call, an email, social media, a text message, a written letter, or an in-person visit are all options. It's up to you to decide how you'll best communicate and how the information is likely to be best received by your family member.

Consider the potential risks and benefits of each one. Showing up on someone's doorstep may work in some cases. In others, it may be too overwhelming or could lead to a heated disagreement.

Communicating via email, text message, or social media, can put less pressure on the other person to respond right away. But your communication may not be as clear when the other person can't hear your tone or see your body language.

A phone call may cause the person to be taken off guard. But hearing your voice may also remind them that they've missed you. Or they may hear in your voice that you're a different person than you were when you became estranged.

**Take Action**

Once you have a plan for how you'll reach out and what you're going to say, it's time to take action. This is also a good time to consider professional support. A trained therapist can be valuable in helping you process the past and establish healthy boundaries as you reconnect with estranged family.

**Reach Out**

You might decide it's best to reach out at a time that has meaning for the both of you. Perhaps you call on a holiday, or maybe you send a letter at a certain time of the year that reminds you of the person. Maybe you just decide to try and establish contact on the day you feel ready to do so.

Take a deep breath and pick up the phone, or send your message. See what happens.

If your first attempt or two go without a response, don't despair. The other person may simply need some more time to think about rekindling the relationship.

Don't overdo it with attempts to contact the other person, however. Calling too many times or sending repeat messages may drive them further away.

## Build Trust Over Time

If your family member responds positively to your contact, move forward with the relationship slowly. Don't expect to pick up where you left off before you became estranged. Instead, build trust one step at a time.

Whether you start communicating by text message only for a while, or you meet for coffee in-person once a month, get to know one another again.

Be a good listener. Validate the other person's feelings, even if you don't understand them.6 Your adult child may insist that you scarred them for life over an incident you don't even recall. Or your sister might claim it's unfair you were always your parents' favorite.

Depending on the reason you became estranged, it may be helpful to establish some rules for this new phase of your relationship. For example, you might want to say, "If our discussion gets heated and you raise your voice, I'm going to end the conversation," or, "I am happy to let you see the children. But if you put me down in front of them, I'll have to end contact."

Your rekindled relationship may go through a bit of a honeymoon phase early on. You might enjoy catching up with one another, and things might seem to go well. But it's common for unresolved issues to start rearing their ugly head at some point down the road. If things get tough, consider getting professional help.

**Get Professional Help**

Whether you decide to get help for yourself so you can establish healthy boundaries, or you decide to go to family therapy to maintain a healthy relationship, professional help can be key to helping you work through issues.

A psychotherapist can assist you with meeting your goals, healing old wounds, improving your communication, and addressing the issues that led to estrangement in the first place. Therapy can help you move forward in a healthy manner.

You might also consider getting professional help if the person you tried to rekindle the relationship with didn't respond to your efforts. Therapy might help you manage the emotions you experience, ranging from grief and confusion to hope and anger.

So, family dynamics are complicated. And deciding to reach out to an estranged family member isn't a decision you should take lightly.

Sometimes it's healthier for everyone to cease contact. But if you decide to try and rekindle the relationship, go slowly. Look at it as an opportunity to learn more about yourself, regardless of the outcome.

# CHAPTER 8

# How to Reconcile With Your Estranged Daughter

If your daughter has cut you out of her life, you may be wondering how to reconcile with your estranged daughter. While reconciliation is never guaranteed, there are healthy steps you can take to better understand the situation and improve your chances of making appropriate contact with her.

One of the most important concepts to understand when considering reconciliation with your daughter is knowing that it may not happen, and if it does, it may not be on your time frame. At some point, you will need to grapple with these notions before moving forward so you aren't driven to force contact with her before she is comfortable doing so.

**Tips if You Have Been Estranged or Cut off From Your Daughter**

Simple tips to keep in mind when considering making contact with your daughter:

- **Respect her boundaries -** if she has asked you not to contact her, give her time until she's ready.
- **Do not ask other people to get involved in the situation and speak on your behalf or pressure her to contact you -** this is totally inappropriate and violates her boundaries, which can push her further away.
- **Do not send gifts or bribe her with money -** this is not a healthy way to make contact with her.
- **Do not contact any of her friends, her place of work, school, or her children and/or immediate family -** again this is an inappropriate boundary violation, which will likely push her away.

- Before diving into a conversation with her, sending her a long text, or leaving her a voicemail, ask her if she's comfortable speaking with you or if she'd like more time.

- If your daughter doesn't respond to your request to speak with her, let her know you respect her decision and am here when she's ready to talk.

- Consider beginning your own individual therapy both for support during this painful situation, as well as an opportunity to increase your insight into the situation.

**Letter to My Estranged Daughter**

If you have decided to write a letter to your daughter in hopes of connecting with her, it's important to take responsibility for your mistakes within the relationship, avoid blaming her or mind-reading why she chose to cut you off, and reinforce the notion that you are committed to respecting her boundaries and want to mend the unhealthy aspects of your relationship. In this type of letter, wording is crucial:

- **Example of parentification (asking her to parent you inappropriately):** "I'm a failure of a parent and this whole mess is my fault. I shouldn't even try any more." In this example, the parent is asking their daughter to take care of them emotionally instead of owning up to their missteps.

- **Example of healthy alternative statements:** "I know I've made mistakes as a parent, and I'm working with a therapist now to better understand my parenting decisions, as well as the history of unhealthy attachment patterns within my own family of origin. While this in no way excuses my behavior towards you growing up, I wanted to let you know that I'm working on becoming more aware of unconscious choices I've made that have negatively impacted you."

- **Example of unhealthy and pressured communication:** "I'm your parent and you need to talk to me. How you are behaving is hurting me and is unacceptable."

- **Example of honoring your daughter's boundaries:** "I want to let you know I can understand your reasons for no longer wanting to speak with me. I am working with a therapist and learning more about unhealthy family patterns that have been in my family system for generations. I will not be making any further contact with you unless you initiate it. I want to give you your space and make sure you know that I am working hard to gain more insight into our relationship. I love you and am here for you if or when you are ready to speak."

## Questions to Ask Your Estranged Daughter

Initial questions you may consider asking your daughter:

- Are you comfortable speaking with me today?
- Can you let me know when you feel comfortable speaking with me in the future? If not, I understand and respect your decision.
- Can you help me understand your perspective?

- Would you consider going to see a therapist with me? I'd love to work on making our relationship healthier.
- Are you comfortable sharing why you decided to no longer speak with me?
- How would you like to communicate with me going forward? I understand if you don't wish to speak at all.
- Would you prefer to speak in person, through text, or on the phone? (if she has agreed to speak with you)

## How Do I Talk to My Estranged Daughter?

If your daughter has agreed to speak with you, it's important to focus on understanding her perspective, without judgment, and refraining from stating your point of view until she feels heard. When speaking with her, use phrases and questions like:

- Thank you so much for speaking with me. I love you so much and really want to understand your point of view.

- I can understand why you feel that way.
- While it's difficult to hear that, I so appreciate you being honest with me about your feelings.
- I am so grateful that you felt comfortable speaking with me today. Would you be open to speaking again?
- Thank you for sharing your perspective. It has really helped me understand my role in your decision to take some time for yourself.
- If she asks you why you made a certain decision, or anything that brings up defensiveness for you, say you need to think about it for a bit, instead of responding in a way that could trigger an argument.
- I am here to listen and really want to understand your point of view.
- Would you be open to doing a therapy session with me?
- What can I do to help you feel heard during this conversation?

- Are you comfortable sharing with me what you need from me going forward? I want to make sure you feel loved and respected by me.

When speaking with your daughter, do not blame her, make yourself the victim (it's my fault, I'm terrible, etc.), or engage in an argument with her. Go into the situation with the perspective that you are there to listen and understand her point of view, and that's it. She may not be in a place to hear your point of view yet, and it's your job as her parent to facilitate an interaction where she feels safe sharing with you.

# CHAPTER 9

# How To Reconnect With a Child You Abandoned

Abandonment is quite tricky to work through as a parent because when it is experienced by a child, it triggers core survival related feelings of unsafety. This feeling of unsafety can lead to unconsciously feeling as if you're going to die, but this will depend on what age the child was when abandoned. If you have decided you want to try to reconnect with your child:

- Understand the weight of how your decisions may have impacted them growing up

- Know that it is up to them if they feel comfortable reconnecting with you and you'll need to be respectful of their choice
- Reach out by first asking if they are comfortable having a conversation instead of assuming they will be
- Ask if it's okay if you check in with them to see how they are doing and how frequently they'd like you to do so
- See if they would be comfortable going to therapy with you to work on your relationship

# CHAPTER 10

# How to Reconcile With Your Estranged Adult Child

Your daughter, now in her 30s, stopped talking to you after you and she had words over finances, a good 10 years ago. You've reached out to her several times since the dispute, eager to mend fences and get your relationship back on track. But your voice mails have not been returned. You feel heartbroken, angry and helpless.

Experts agree that there seems to be an increase in separations between adult children and one or both of their parents. One survey of more than 800 British adults who self-identify as partly or fully estranged from one or both parents found that it's more often the adult child who initiates the separation. The study reported that more daughters than sons initiate breakups. Further, more mothers than fathers are estranged from their adult kids. Estrangement from fathers, however, lasts longer: an average of 7.9 years, compared with 5.5 years from mothers.

While the survey found that a sizable majority of adult kids don't expect reconciliation, some parents see glimmers of hope and believe that, with the right approach, they can find a way back into the relationship. But there are right ways and wrong ways to handle a possible reconciliation.

## Dos and Don'ts of Reconciliation

- Do handwrite a note or leave a brief voice mail.
- Do approach the situation lightly.
- Do reach out infrequently but authentically.
- Do apologize.
- Don't text or email.
- Don't get into a big explanation.
- Don't allow silence to take over.
- Don't plead your case.

There are as many reasons as there are stories for these breakups. The website *We Have Kids* lists a few common ones: conflict with the child's partner, resentment over parents' divorce, an adult child's difficulties with how her parents are grandparenting, longtime parental lack of nurturing, or boundary-breaking behavior. Sometimes there's been an episode that causes a break; other times, and more likely, long-simmering issues are triggered by a smaller concern.

**Don't rehash the past**

Experts in family dynamics recommend specific ways to reach out as well as what to avoid doing. Bonnie Cushing, a clinical social worker in Montclair, New Jersey, who counsels families as part of her practice, advises parents not to text or email their estranged child, but "a hand-written note is a beautiful way to initiate reconciliation." If a note is not your style, then leave a brief message on your child's voice mail.

## Stay simple

Don't get into the whys and wherefores of the situation. Just say that you're interested in reconnecting and ask if he is ready.

Cushing observes that sometimes when parents try to bridge the gap, they come on too strong, explain too much or assert their own version of the breakup story. Often the adult child gets the sense that the attempts at reaching out are all about healing the parent, Cushing says. Bringing the grandchildren into the conversation is another nonstarter that muddies the waters. "Again, it makes it seem like it's all about the parent and their needs," she says. "It's better to switch the focus, where the parent [takes some responsibility]."

## Keep the door open

But if you're not sure when or if you'll get an opening for an apology, at the very least you can bridge the gap, with no strings attached. Rather than "allow the silence to seep in, you can maintain a respectful connection with infrequent but authentic reach-outs," Cushing says. This tells your child that "as long as I'm alive, we're connected." While you may not reconnect in the way you'd like, you've demonstrated that you care.

Estranged siblings and friends should heed the same advice. Unless there has been serious abuse, physical or otherwise, an effort toward reconnection of some sort is often advised. Petty grievances should not be allowed to prevent reconciliation once there has been a cooling-off period.

**Set realistic expectations**

All parents make mistakes, McGregor says. "Most adults, including parents of estranged adult children, can identify things we thought our own parents didn't handle well or things we planned to do differently with our own children." At the same time, keep your own needs in mind. "Sometimes I hear from parents who say they'd do anything to have their son or daughter back," she says. "That attitude isn't healthy because it sets up an inequitable relationship."

In reaching out, you'd do well to lower your expectations. McGregor warns not to assume there will be a positive change. "Too often, parents receive a text, reply to it and then hear nothing more. If they try to arrange a meeting, it may be ignored." In fact, the British study reported the crushing statistic that more than 70 percent of adult kids say they don't expect or plan on a reconciliation. Sometimes "giving in to an adult child's decision is the only sensible choice," McGregor says.

The fact is, any reconciliation will take effort, patience and strength. Instead of pinning all your hopes on a potential text, "don't let the estrangement define you or your life," she advises. "Help yourself now and you'll be better prepared if or when a reconciliation comes about." McGregor recommends refocusing your attention on yourself and your family outside of the estranged child, reaching out to others and taking an active hand in shaping your future.

"One golden rule," says Cushing, "is based on the principle that a cutoff is not really a cutoff unless both parties co-sign on it."

**How parents reconnect with estranged daughters or sons?**

Reconnecting with an estranged family member can bring a lot of past emotions to the surface. For one, if you're looking to reconnect with a child who has disconnected from you, it might challenging. Also, gear up for a long term journey. It has taken many years to create the disconnection and hostility. So, it will take lots of time and little moments of nurturing to rebuild connection and a meaningful relationship.

**How to write a letter to your estranged child (that you won't actually give to them)**

To begin, write this letter as if you were going to write to your daughter, who you miss so deeply. But, do you not actually mail this letter. Letter writing helps parents reconnect with estranged daughters or sons by building self-connection and self-awareness. Now, this is more of an exercise for you to get clear on what type of relationship you would like moving forward. For instance, you may say, "I am so sorry. I wish I could have been there more for you when you were younger."

Notice yourself when it comes to reconnecting your relationship with your estranged daughter or son

Now, this experience of reconnecting with your estranged daughter or son is not actually about getting a relationship back. Instead, think of this as a journey of healing all of the unhealed parts of yourself. For instance, the parts of you that get angry really easily and fly off the handle with hostility. Also, notice the part of you that might be emotionally shaming to your daughter or not want the tears. Perhaps, there was a time when your son or daughter was crying and you made her feel ashamed for being emotional. Moments like this might have very little impact on you as a parent. But, the experience of reconnecting with your estranged daughter or son is not actually about getting a relationship back. But, a child's mind may hold onto very specific, traumatic memories as part of the root of the cut off or grudge.

**Talk about issues without getting defensive**

If your son or daughter wants to talk about the past, just listen. Also, talking about these issues will be a very big step in rebuilding a healthy loving relationship. Remember, it is always okay to cry. Really, crying is a beautiful part of healing anger and showing vulnerability. As a parent, crying can help your adult child see you are human too. To note, daughters and sons often hold anger, hostility, and choose to become estranged as a result of unhealed traumatic wound.

**Book a phone consult for positive coping skills today.**

Focus on build emotional closeness, not buying love

Also, it might feel easy to try to offer your estranged child or young adult money. However, I would encourage you to forgo offering money. Unfortunately, offering money can make your child feel like you're buying their love. Often times, and emotional, meaningful connection can help heal a thousand times over. See if you can text or email your son or daughter. As a parent, you may need to be the one to take initiative and text your child every morning. Also, your adult child may not respond, but keep the communication going. Even if it is one way, they receive them. Your son or daughter may also be testing you to see if you will give up easily.

**What to share when you are a parent reconnecting with estranged daughters or sons**

I would recommend bringing up a positive childhood memory that you can share, that brought you both joy. So, text a memory of this event or email in memory of this positive, fun event to your son or daughter. Focusing on a positive past memory can help to rebuild a connection with an estranged daughter or son. Remember, don't start by going into deep, past issues. Essentially, keep your messages about positive, happy, confident moment at first.

## Apologize first

As a parent, it's important to take accountability for your anger, past traumas, and behaviors. Remember, you may need to be humble and take a step down. Also, apologize for any type of challenging moments from the past. Perhaps, there was a moment in your parenting where you had an addiction or alcoholism that challenged your family and your children. Or, perhaps you had bipolar disorder and that impacted your family. Apologizing for any past hurt not only liberate yourself. But, apologizing shows your child that you are willing to do what it takes to have a meaningful relationship. Lastly, a true, meaningful relationship is about repairing and healing after past hurt and betrayal.

Take time to mourn the loss if you are a parents who can't reconnect with an estranged daughters or sons

Also, if your son or daughter has completely cut you off and will no longer connect or speak with you, take time to mourn the loss. Essentially, this is a loss just like a death in the family and the grieving process. So, take time to cry.

Crying is always okay. Also, journal about the loss of relationship.

**Adopt another young adult as your son or daughter**

To add, be resilient. See if you can find someone in your neighborhood or in your town that can be a an adopted daughter or son. Often, emerging young adults need guidance from mature older adults. Remember, keep sharing your love and positivity. For instance, is a young adult that lives near you that needs a loving parent? And, can offer your love to that emerging young adult in the form of positive energy?

**Parents reconnect with estranged daughters or sons can seek individual counseling**

If your son or daughter has cut you off, choose to focus on yourself through counseling or telehealth. Furthermore, counseling can help you come to terms with the past. And, individual counseling can help you gain clarity around your relationship with your estranged son or daughter. Family therapy can help you understand your behaviors and a role in the parent-child relationship. Lastly, counseling can also help you prepare for reconnecting and help you prevent making the same mistakes you did in the past, which caused the cut off.

# CHAPTER 11

# Estranged from Your Adult Child? Things You Can Do

If you are estranged from your adult child, if your child has cut you out of his or her life—whether for a long or short time—it is a gut-wrenching experience. When your child cuts you out of her life it provokes deep feelings of shame, guilt, bewilderment, and hurt, all of which can easily turn to anger. On top of that, it can also arouse people's worst suspicions (surely, the Jones' must be terrible parents for their daughter to cut them off like that!) and leave you feeling judged, even by friends and family.

Sometimes, of course, there are circumstances in which cutting off from a parent is the only viable option for an adult child (age 18 and older), for instance, in the case of past or present physical, emotional or sexual abuse from a parent.

While it's common to pin the reason for the estrangement on everything from money issues, to personality conflicts, to divorce or difficult family dynamics, many times, though, estranged parents are left in the dark trying to figure out what went wrong.

And when you are in the dark, the easiest thing to blame is yourself—to believe that you failed as a parent.

But here's the reality: it was not your choice to sever the relationship. Although you may have contributed to the tensions between you, you are not responsible for your child's choice to cut you off.

Many adult children struggle with their parents, or with money issues, etc., but not all of them cut ties with their parents. Why do some cut off while others go through similar struggles and stay connected?

## Why Some Kids Distance Themselves

We humans manage stress in pretty predictable ways. We have a fight or flight response just like other species. And some people are more prone to distancing (flight) when emotional intensity gets high.

Let's take Joe, for example. Joe was living at home after college, and his parents felt he was aimless. He would sleep in late, not help around the house, wouldn't get a steady job, and was rude and disrespectful.

Joe's parents were understandably concerned and anxious about his lack of direction. They would nag, yell, and question him daily as to his game plan. He would be vague or get nasty, which caused his parents to get on his back even more.

Eventually, Joe moved out. He didn't tell his parents where he moved and didn't contact them for over a year.

To understand Joe's response, we have to recognize that when some people feel anxious, tired of conflict or pressure, or too much of the sticky family togetherness, their response is to distance themselves, be it emotionally, physically or both. When a person distances from others, they feel a sense of relief because the distance seemingly brings the conflict to an end. Of course, nothing is actually resolved; instead, more stress is generated.

On the outside, it looks as though Joe and his parents are disconnected. But on the inside, they are actually thinking about each other all the time and remain overly focused on one another. They are, in fact, still extremely involved with one another: they are emotionally bound up together, even though all communication has ceased. Neither is free from the original problem; nor are they free from each other.

**Extreme Distancing: Cutting Off**

Distancing, at its extreme, turns to cutting off. It can occur after long periods of conflict or as a sudden reaction to a difficult encounter. Whatever the issue, the person doing the cutting off has difficulty addressing and resolving the problem directly and maturely. Instead, like Joe, they stop communicating. Continuing the relationship seems unmanageable to them.

When a parent and child are too emotionally bound up with each other, they are more susceptible to cutting off when anxiety is high.

Joe and his parents, for instance, were overly involved and entangled with each other. He was not taking responsibility for himself, nor were his parents taking responsibility for themselves.

His parents did not stand up and let him know what they would and wouldn't accept. Instead they nagged, begged and hoped he would change. He dug his heels in deeper, did less when pushed, and refused to address his part of the problem.

They were living in reaction to one another, rather than each taking responsibility for their part of the family conflict. The only way that Joe could see to solve the problem was to distance himself and eventually cut-off from his parents; Joe didn't have the skills necessary to untie the knots, to grow up and face himself.

Parents feel powerless when no contact is possible, when they can't negotiate or even talk with their child. Should you contact your child or not? How long should you try? What should you say?

## Five Tips When Estranged and Cut Off From Your Child

### Get Support

Being cut off by your child, with no ability to understand, communicate and resolve things, is difficult enough. That's why being connected to others who love and understand you is particularly important. In addition to reaching out to friends and family, consider joining a support group. If you are not able to function at your best, get some professional help.

### Don't Cut off in Response

You are not the one cutting ties; your child is. Don't cut off your child in response. Continue to reach out to him, letting him know that you love him and that you want to mend whatever has broken. Send birthday and holiday messages as well as occasional brief notes or emails. Simply say that you are thinking about him and hope to have the opportunity to reconnect. Send your warmth, love and compassion—as you get on with your life.

## Don't Feed the Anger

It's understandable to feel angry. And in their attempt to be supportive, friends and family may fuel your feelings of betrayal, inadvertently increasing your anger. Anger is natural, but not helpful. Step back and try to understand what led to this estrangement. What patterns were operating in your family dance? If you can look at your family from a more factual vantage point, it may feel less personal. No one is to blame. Now if the door opens, you will be in a much better position to reconcile.

## Listen to Your Child Without Defending Yourself

If the door opens with your child, listen with an open heart. Listen to her perceptions of what wrongs took place. Even if you disagree with her, look for the grains of truth. Be willing to look at yourself. It's hard to hear these criticisms, especially if your intentions were misunderstood. So prepare yourself to handle this. Your adult child may need to hold on to blame as a way to manage her own anxiety. Just letting her know that you hear her will go a long way. Keep in mind that she, too, had to be in tremendous pain to reach the point of shutting you out. Try to empathize with her pain rather than get caught up in the hurt and anger.

## Focus on Yourself, Not Your Child

If you do begin communicating again, you will be in a position to learn from the mistakes of the past and work toward an improved relationship. Put your efforts into changing yourself, not your child. Let go of your resentments regarding the estrangement. Understand his need to flee—and forgive him.

## Understanding and Hope

Get to know the adult child you have, not the child you think he should have been. Allow him to get to know you. If your child still has made no contact, grieve the loss and know there is still hope. Try to manage your anxiety, and do the right thing by staying in touch with him in a non-intrusive way: occasionally and lovingly. Things may change.

Rather than blame yourself or your child for this pain, use your energy to learn about yourself, your own family history and patterns in your other relationships. Look for other patterns of cutting off in your family tree.

Remember that shutting a person out is a response to anxiety and a family that is overly entangled with one another. Your actions or lack of action didn't cause this. Cutting off is a way people manage anxiety when they don't know a better way. The love and caring is there; the ability to solve differences is not. You did not make your child to turn away. That was her decision. It may have been a poor one, but it was the best she could do at the time. Try to get your focus off of her at least 50 percent of the day, which will make a difference.

Your pain is real. Be mindful and compassionate of it, but don't allow it to define or overwhelm you. Put the focus on what you have control of: your own life.

# CHAPTER 12

# What to do if your child has rejected you

Being estranged from your kid is painful and can make you feel like a bad parent. But there may be a way to mend the rift.

For example, for Rick and his son Peter, the trouble began during Peter's high school years.

By his own description, Rick was a strict parent; Peter a rebel, dabbling in drinking and drugs. In response, Rick grounded him, often, and took away his allowance. When Peter was arrested for underage drinking, Rick didn't come bail him out. "In my book, that's tough love and what a good parent does," he says.

When Peter left for college, however, the parent-child relationship took a turn. The two haven't spoken for over five years. "A gulf opened up between us," says Rick, 64, "He never forgave me and won't; says it was clear I didn't love him.

"Peter insists it's better for his mental state if we only exchange holiday cards once a year, which breaks my heart. His absence from my life and my feelings of failure — those are with me daily."

A not-so-uncommon state of affairs

The definition of estrangement, experts say, is a "prolonged" period of detachment or distancing — with little or extremely limited contact. The time period in question can vary between family members, depending on what their relationship and frequency of contact was to begin with.

As many as 20% to 25% of people may have some form of estrangement in their family.

And while estrangement might seem extreme, it's probably more common that you think. Parent-child estrangement occurs in about one out of 10 families, according to Megan Gilligan, PhD, professor of Human Development and Family Studies at Iowa State University, who has done ground-breaking research in this realm.

But when you factor in sibling estrangement in addition to the parent-child variety — and the fact that many estranged family members don't like to discuss this kind of distancing — as many as 20% to 25% of people may have some form of estrangement in their family, says Kristina Scharp, Ph.D., an assistant professor in the Department of Communication at the University of Washington, who also studies estrangement.

**How families split**

In the movie version of estrangement, there's a big blow-up that ends in a dramatic "we're not speaking" type of proclamation.

In reality, estrangement is often a more gradual process. Typically, there are issues between parents and children (or siblings), that don't get addressed and fester over time.

The estrangement is typically set into motion by an adult child at a critical rite of passage — a teenager leaving home for college, taking on a full-time job, or entering a serious relationship, and then communication gets sparse.

Often the estranged parent will remark, 'Gosh, how long has it actually been since we've spoken...let me think about it,'. "That's what we usually hear, with the parent being surprised at how much time has passed."

Said one father, "I accept that my son is gay, and I love him, but given the religious views I was raised with, it's uncomfortable for me to hear about his boyfriends, so I don't call often and inquire about his life. And I think he gets it and doesn't call me much either."

But even when the process of estrangement is gradual, the arrangement rarely lacks for rancor.

## The prospect of mending fences

If you're looking to heal a family rift, the sooner the better. Before you reach out, however, you need to look in. If you're feeling defensive, or unwilling to accept some of the blame, the odds of a reconciliation are low.

"It's tempting to blame your child for being too sensitive, unreasonable, or not forgiving enough, especially when it's not clear what the problem is.

But attempts to reconcile rely on openness to feedback and a willingness to apologize, even if you didn't intend any harm or realize there was a problem. You don't have to agree with your child's version of events, but if you want to be close again, you must be able to at least grasp your child's point of view and offer a heartfelt apology.

## Offering the olive branch

Reconnecting is a delicate dance. You don't want to appear demanding (and you never want to issue an ultimatum). But you also don't want to be so passive that you seem not to care.

Be specific about next steps. Lots of parents suggest to their child, 'Why don't we go out for lunch some time?' and then feel hurt when the child doesn't initiate.' Are you free for lunch on this particular date at this restaurant at this time?' is more manageable than a general request for more togetherness.

Don't blame third parties. It's not uncommon for estrangement to go hand in hand with your child getting deeply involved in another relationship.

That's what happened to Arlene, 70. "My son and I were always so close, but since he got married, how things have changed!" she says. "His wife doesn't like me; he says she feels I am 'critical.' She keeps herself and my son booked up on the weekends so there's no chance to join us for dinner. I haven't actually laid eyes on him in months. What if that becomes years?"

Chances are, though, that your child's current relationship isn't the root of the problem. "It's not so common to have your child's mind taken over by another person.

Stop focusing on the daughter-in-law and figure out where you are with your son. Offer a real apology for the current situation and try to move forward.

Invite a professional to the conversation. If your child is willing, airing the situation in front of family therapist can help you understand other perspectives and offer tools for better communication. It also shows your commitment to changing the situation.

**Knowing when to let go**

There may also be times when it's better to accept the rift and even embrace it, experts say. When the relationship is abusive, or is damaging other family members, you might need to consider alternatives.

Estrangement can be a healthy solution to an unhealthy environment rather than a sad, terrible experience.

The roles, support, and affection a family should provide can be found elsewhere. You can have what's called 'voluntary kin' and create your own family.

# CHAPTER 13

# How to Deepen Empathy with Your Estranged Child

If your adult child has stopped communicating, and their love seems to be long gone, don't lose hope. A key step in healing estrangement occurs when parents bring empathy and compassion to the forefront of this fractured relationship.

Both in my capacity as a therapist and as a regular citizen, I've talked with adults who are struggling with the decision to cut ties with their parents, have already done so, or have recently reconciled with a formerly rejected parent. I've also followed the research that studies the feelings and motivations of these adult children. By all accounts, these folks take parental estrangement seriously. They feel weighed down by it. It hurts them profoundly to lose connection with a parent, even by their own choice.

Here's what one estranged child wrote in response to one post:

*It is awful when you choose to end a relationship...especially when your parent doesn't (maybe even can't) understand what they did wrong. To turn away from them in order to move forward as a healthier person feels absolutely selfish and goes against my instincts to maintain that connection with my mother.*

I've heard similar expressions of dismay from my clients, friends, and colleagues who reluctantly avoid their parents. Everyone wants to have parents they love, and who love them back, without chronic trouble or pain between them.

**It Cuts Both Ways**

Most parents don't get to see the vulnerability and unhappiness in their distancing child. Instead, they're presented only with heated rejection or chilly indifference. No wonder they're sometimes ready to believe they created a monster.

We humans are at our most hurtful to others—our most "monstrous"—when we're in pain ourselves. As the saying goes, hurt people hurt people. It makes sense that your child's rejection, coming as it does from a place of pain, will also be hurtful to you.

You and your estranged child also share the task of explaining to friends why you won't be getting together with the family for the holidays this year. Believe it or not, it's the same awkward conversation for him that it is for you. Estranged adult children, for the most part, feel unsupported when they share the sensitive information that they're estranged from you. Friends, relatives, and society all pressure them to reconcile.

It makes sense that your child's rejection, coming as it does from a place of pain, will also be hurtful to you.

It's clear that the vast majority of estrangers do not cut ties with their parents on a whim, for purely materialistic reasons, or just because someone else tells them to. So—please don't let me lose you here—contact with Mom or Dad has to be pretty darn painful to be worse than no contact. Don't worry: it's not necessarily as bad as it sounds, and the situation can potentially be mended if you keep an open mind. Let me share some encouraging words from a mom who's now reconnected with her formerly estranged daughter:

I didn't know what to do, and couldn't work out why my daughter was so angry and hostile towards me, and didn't initiate any contact. I can now appreciate how complex the situation was, and feel able to look at our estrangement more from her perspective.

You and your estranged child are both in uncharted waters; he may not have the words to tell you what went wrong or what he'd like you to do about it. Even if he does, he might use language or examples that only confuse you and leave you feeling helpless.

## The Healing Power of Awareness

Whether or not the estrangement is acrimonious, many parents become defensive when their adult children don't want to maintain contact. Shame and defensiveness are the enemies of awareness. And unfortunately, there can be no movement, no change, and no healing without awareness.

Shame says, "I don't want to know if I did anything to deserve this; it's too painful to feel that bad about myself." Awareness says, "I want to understand my part in this, even if it's painful."

In order to recover a relationship with your child, you must find a way to put shame aside and invite compassion into your heart. You need to tolerate looking at whatever your child may want to show you if healing is to occur. If there is something important for you to learn about the way your child experiences you, you won't be able to see it through a cloud of shame.

In order to recover a relationship with your child, you must find a way to put shame aside and invite compassion into your heart.

You have no option for a considered response as long as shame and defensiveness have you in their grip. Breaking free of these can pave the way for a closer, calmer, and more honest relationship with your child.

Made in United States
Troutdale, OR
04/05/2024

18953886R10080